A FIRST BOOK

YOUR IMMUNE SYSTEM

BY ALAN E. NOURSE, M.D.

FRANKLIN WATTS

NEW YORK | LONDON | TORONTO | SYDNEY | 1982

Photographs courtesy of
The Center for Disease Control, Atlanta, Georgia:
pp. 8 (both), 11 (bottom), 25 (top), 41, 42;
Carolina Biological Supply Co.: p. 11 (top);
The Free Library of Philadelphia: pp. 12, 37, 38;
Taurus Photos: pp. 19 (both), 25 (bottom);
American Cancer Society: p. 55.

Diagrams courtesy of Vantage Art, Inc.

Library of Congress Cataloging in Publication Data

Nourse, Alan Edward.
Your immune system.

(A First book)
Bibliography: p.
Includes index.
Summary: Discusses the workings of the body's
immune defense system; what happens when this
system functions perfectly, too vigorously, or not at all;
and current research in immunology.
1. Immunology—Juvenile literature.
[1. Immunology] I. Title.
QR181.8.N68 1982   612.07'9   82-8456
ISBN 0-531-04462-9   AACR2

CONTENTS

YOUR IMMUNE SYSTEM

YOUR IMMUNE DEFENSE SYSTEM

Would you believe that lurking beneath the quiet surface of your body you have a ferocious army of defenders busily fighting grim, life-or-death battles, day and night, to protect you from alien invaders?

That's not just a science fiction story. It's the truth. That protective army is your natural *immune defense system* (usually just called the *immune system*), and the scientific study of the way it works is known as *immunology*. Your immune system began fighting for your life soon after you were born, and—if all goes well—it will continue fighting for you until you die. It keeps working whether you are sick or well, happy or sad, awake or asleep. When it doesn't work properly, you can become very ill indeed. But as long as it protects you as it should, you remain healthy in the midst of terrible dangers.

Protects you? From what? From an amazing variety of things in the world around you that don't belong inside your body. Your immune system's primary task is to keep you alive, and it does that job remarkably well. If you didn't have an immune system, you might have to live in a strange, artificial world like the little boy we will call Bobby L.

A BODY WITHOUT DEFENSES

Not long ago Bobby L. celebrated his tenth birthday, and for him that was something of a miracle. Soon after he was born, Bobby had to be sealed inside a completely airtight, germ-free plastic incubator. From then on, nothing from the world outside could be allowed to come in contact with him without first being carefully treated to make it germ-free. He could not be allowed to touch another human being, not even his own parents. As he grew, he had to have larger and larger plastic "houses" in which to live. He could only go outside his germ-free cage by dressing in a plastic "space suit," like a moon-walking astronaut. On his tenth birthday his parents and friends were on hand to celebrate—but they all had to stay *outside* his plastic barrier.

Why couldn't Bobby L. live like other people? There was nothing wrong with his environment, but there was something very wrong with Bobby. While his body was developing before birth, an important part of Bobby was left out—the immune defense system we spoke of earlier. He had no protective army inside him, fighting to keep him alive—none at all.

Doctors speak of Bobby's rare disorder as *combined immunodeficiency disease*. All this means is that Bobby's body has no natural protection against the alien invaders—including the bacteria and viruses—that surround us on all sides. Nor is there any way, at the present time, anyhow, to supply Bobby with the immune protection his body lacks. When it isn't present naturally, there is just no substitute for it.

What would happen if this boy were to go outside his germ-free plastic house and try to live like the rest of us? Very soon he would be sick with a cold, a sore throat, or an earache—and the illness would linger on and on. He would go from one infection to another in spite of antibiotics or other treatment, until finally one infection would become so severe that medicines wouldn't be able to control it and he would die. He might survive a couple of months or years outside his germ-free house, but not much longer. Perhaps someday doctors may learn how to overcome the sort of immune deficiency Bobby suffers from, but so far there is no effective treatment. For now, at least, he must remain inside his protected, sealed-off world.

THE OTHER SIDE OF THE PICTURE

Fortunately, Bobby's kind of immuno-deficiency disease is extremely rare. Most people have a perfectly normal, fully active immune system working for them all their lives. In fact, many people have problems not because they lack immune defenses, but because their immune systems are working a little too vigorously.

Mary Sue K. has such a problem. One April morning every year she wakes up sneezing violently, her eyes red, her nose itching. For the next two weeks her nose will run constantly, her ears will itch, and she will sneeze and sneeze and sneeze. A special antihistamine medicine will clear up her symptoms for a few hours at a time, but they return as soon as the medicine wears off. Then about two weeks after they start, the symptoms go away all by themselves just as suddenly and mysteriously as they began.

Mary Sue's doctor says that she has "hay fever" due to an allergic reaction to maple tree pollen. (No other pollen bothers her.) During her attacks the moist inner lining of her nose becomes clogged with a special kind of white blood cell not normally present in such large numbers. This is a telltale sign that her immune system is fiercely *overreacting* to contact with an "alien invader"—the offending pollen—and that is exactly what an allergic reaction is. By starting a long series of injections in the middle of the winter to make her body less sensitive to the pollen, Mary Sue might avoid her hay fever attack the next spring, but she prefers just to take the antihistamines for relief until the pollen goes away and the symptoms disappear on their own.

Mary Sue's hay fever is mostly just a nuisance. She is one of millions of people who have minor allergic reactions to various foreign substances they come in contact with. But Roger M., a ninth-grader, has a more serious allergic problem. Since the age of six he has had periodic attacks of asthma, a respiratory disease in which the tiny air tubes in the lungs squeeze shut, trapping air inside and forcing the victim to struggle and wheeze trying to push the air out again. Roger's asthma attacks begin quite suddenly and without warning. First his chest begins to feel tight. A few moments later he is fighting for breath, coughing and wheezing. Without the proper medicine, the attack might last all day or all night, leaving him exhausted. To prevent this, he must take pills every day to help keep his air tubules relaxed; this helps prevent attacks.

Asthma is not always caused by allergies; it can arise from

many different sources. But in Roger's case, his asthma is the result of an allergic reaction to the mold spores that are found in ordinary house dust. To help him avoid contact with these "alien invaders," Roger's bedroom is now fitted with special air filters, and everyone in his family works hard to keep dust from accumulating. His asthma attacks are never life-threatening, and they always go away sooner or later, but they are a thoroughly frightening and unpleasant health problem just the same. Unfortunately, Roger may have asthma for the rest of his life. His natural immune system is working so hard protecting him from a foreign substance—mold spores—that it actually makes him far more sick than the mold spores alone could possibly make him.

At the age of thirteen Kathy D. had an even more frightening allergic problem. Kathy didn't think she was allergic to anything until one day at summer camp when she was stung by a bee—and thought she was going to die as a result of it. Within three minutes her eyelids grew puffy, and huge, itchy bumps appeared all over her body. A few moments later her voice went hoarse, breathing became difficult, and she almost passed out. Fortunately, the camp nurse recognized what was happening and injected her with a medicine called Adrenalin to quiet the attack long enough to get the girl to a nearby hospital emergency room. There other treatment restored Kathy's abnormally low blood pressure and soon put an end to her sudden and frightening attack. The doctor said she had suffered an anaphylactic shock—a sudden, massive overreaction of her body's immune system to an alien invader (in this case the venom from a bee sting). On very rare occasions, some people can have similar violent allergic reactions to penicillin, horse serum, or other medicines. Fortunately, such severe reactions to bee stings are so very rare that the average person doesn't have to worry much—most people have only a little harmless burning and swelling after a sting. But when it does occur, such a severe reaction can be very dangerous unless the proper medicine is available and quickly administered. Now Kathy is undergoing treatment to make her body less sensitive to bee venom so the next bee sting will not affect her so seriously.

In the last three cases above, the body's immune system has been overdoing its job of protecting these young people against the invasion of relatively trivial foreign substances. Usually allergies are just a minor nuisance, but in some people they become serious health problems, and on occasion they may even threaten life. But in each case the same basic sequence of events has occurred. First, some foreign substance has found entry into the body. Next, in sharp response, the immune system has sprung into action against the invader and—in these cases—has done its job too well.

Obviously the immune system can be a two-edged weapon. When it isn't working at all, people like Bobby L. can get sick and die. When it does its job too well, people can also get sick. But overall, the immune system is a terribly important and very complex part of the body's normal, everyday functioning. It exists for a real and vital purpose. And although many people experience annoying allergic reactions of one sort or another sometime in their lives, the immune system for the most part does its protective work quietly and unobtrusively—and we survive because of it.

But what, exactly, *is* the body's immune defense system? What is its job, and how does it do it? What are these "alien invaders" it protects us from? To find answers to these questions, we must first see what scientists have learned, bit by bit over the years, about this complex and amazing internal defense system.

ANTIGENS AND ANTIBODIES

Ever since the microscope was invented, over 250 years ago, scientists have realized that we live in a world teeming with tiny living organisms far too small to be seen with the naked eye. They are in the air we breathe, the ground we walk on, the water of our lakes and ponds. They are found on every object we touch, in the clothes we wear, and all over the surface of our bodies. These so-called microorganisms include bacteria (one-celled plantlike organisms); tiny animallike organisms called protozoa; fungi (another kind of simple plant life); and multitudes of different viruses.

Fortunately for us, most of these microorganisms are quite harmless. Many actually do useful things, such as decaying dead vegetation or animals or helping us to digest and absorb our food and get rid of waste materials. But some, once they gain a foothold inside of us, can grow and multiply and cause dangerous infectious diseases. A few, such as the influenza virus or the salmonella bacteria that cause food poisoning, merely make us temporarily ill. But

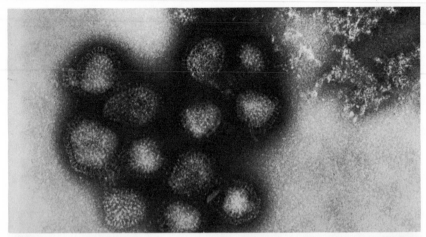

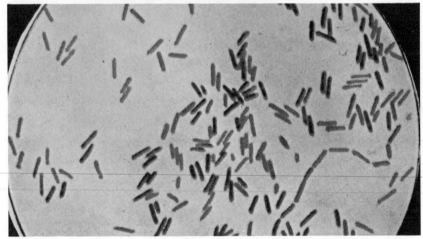

Our bodies are constantly being bombarded by a multitude of microorganisms, some of which can be quite dangerous. Above is an electronmicrograph of an influenza virus of the type that causes the Hong Kong flu. Below is a photomicrograph of the salmonella bacteria that causes food poisoning.

others—such as the polio viruses, the tetanus (lockjaw) bacteria, or the streptococci organisms—can easily cripple or even kill us if they just get the chance. If our bodies did not have some kind of built-in protection against these potential killers, the world would be a very dangerous place to live in, and we would not last long in it.

Of course, the skin covering our bodies helps to keep these organisms out. But the warm, moist membranes inside our noses and throats, our intestinal tracts, and our lungs, for instance, provide these invaders with easy entry. Invaders can also enter the body through cuts and abrasions in the skin. And once inside, they can travel in the bloodstream to cause destructive infections in the brain, lungs, spinal cord, kidneys, urinary bladder, intestine, or any other organ. Viruses actually invade the cells themselves and can ultimately destroy nerve, brain, or lung tissue. What is more, the human body is just the right temperature for these organisms to grow in and is full of nutrients on which they can feed.

In short, without some kind of internal protection we would be coming down with dangerous infections almost constantly. The fact that we ordinarily have only occasional infections, and then usually get over them, tells us that we *do* have a natural protective system that keeps these microorganisms from overwhelming us. We call that internal protective system the immune system.

THE NICE PHAGOCYTES

Most of what we know about our immune system has been learned only in the last twenty or twenty-five years. But a few parts of the picture were pieced together more than ninety years ago. As early as 1888, for example, a Russian biologist named Elie Metchnikoff, working in Paris, discovered that blood contains not only the red blood cells that were seen under the earliest microscopes but also a number of much larger, colorless cells—the white blood cells. These amoebalike white cells seemed to roam about the body at random, scooping up bits of cellular debris and other cast-off materials, for all the world like tiny garbage collectors. They also seemed to scoop up infectious bacteria they encountered in their wanderings—and eat them! Metchnikoff called these white cells *phagocytes*, from Greek words meaning "cells that eat." It soon became clear that whenever a bacterial infection started somewhere in the body, these "nice phagocytes," as Metchnikoff described them, would quickly gather in the area in great numbers and begin battling the bacteria, destroying many of the invaders on the spot—and being destroyed themselves in turn. In fact, the pus that often formed in an infected area was found to be made up largely of dead white blood cells along with millions of dead bacteria. One type of white cell was even larger than the others and did an even better job of killing bacteria. Metchnikoff called these cells *macrophages*, or "big eaters."

About the time Metchnikoff was studying his "nice phago-cytes" another biologist, a man named Emil von Behring, was discovering that people who had survived an attack of diphtheria had some kind of chemical substance in their blood serum (the fluid part of the blood) that was capable of neutralizing a vicious poison, or toxin, given off by the diphtheria bacilli. People who had never been infected with diphtheria had none of this so-called *antitoxin* in their blood. On the heels of this discovery, in the 1890s, other scientists found that many people had other substances in the blood—not phagocytes, but some kind of dissolved chemical substances—that seemed capable of destroying bacteria. Thus, as early as 1900 it was recognized that the human body actually possessed two differ-ent kinds of built-in protection against invading microorganisms: a

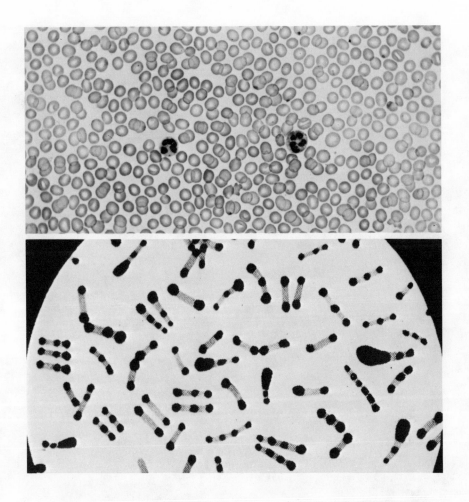

Above: normal human blood, showing red and white blood cells. The dark spots show where phagocytes have gathered at an infection site to destroy invaders. Below: a photomicrograph of diphtheria bacilli. Von Behring discovered that after exposure to diphtheria, the body produces a substance capable of neutralizing the bacteria's toxic effect.

*Russian biologist Elie Metchnikoff discovered in the blood
the presence of white cells that he called phagocytes.*

cellular defense system made up of Metchnikoff's phagocytes and macrophages, and a *serum defense system* (now called the *humoral defense system*), which included both antitoxins that neutralized bacterial poisons and other chemical substances floating in the bloodstream that seemed to destroy bacteria.

THE ANTIBODY ARMY

What exactly were those "other chemical substances" in the bloodstream? For many years nobody knew for sure. Then in the 1930s, laboratory scientists devised a way to separate out individual kinds of proteins from among the many different kinds that form the major building blocks of our organs and tissues. Since then, researchers have learned a great deal about these "other substances" and how they behave when faced by alien invaders such as bacteria or viruses.

First of all, these substances proved to be exactly the same sort of chemicals as the antitoxins, except that they seemed to affect bacteria or viruses instead of toxins. Both of them were special protein molecules that would appear in the bloodstream in enormous numbers shortly after bacteria, bacterial poisons, or viruses had invaded the body. The exact physical shape that these protein molecules took was found to be extremely interesting. In each different invasion they seemed to be carefully form-fitted or shaped to match certain *surface-marker molecules* found on the surface of the invading microorganisms or poisons. In each case, these special serum proteins would fit one—and only one—type of surface-marker molecule, like keys built especially to fit one—and only one—lock. Because they seemed to be made to order—to fit perfectly and attach themselves to the surface-marker molecules on specific invading organisms or poisons—they all came to be called *antibodies*. Once attached to the outside surface of invading organisms, the antibodies seemed to make it easier for the phagocytes to eat them. Because the individual surface-marker molecules on these organisms seemed to be what stimulated or triggered the manufacture of specially shaped antibodies, they came to be spoken of as "anti(body)-generators," or *antigens*. (See Figure 1.)

IMMUNOGLOBULINS ON THE MARCH

All these antibody proteins seem to have certain things in common. All of them, for example, belong to a class of proteins known as *gamma globulins*. Because these proteins seemed to be involved in our immune defense system, scientists called them *immunoglobulins*—"Ig's" for short. Soon it was found that there were several different families of Ig's. One family, known as immunoglobulin A, or IgA, was made up of rather large, clumsy protein molecules that always seemed to appear in the body's fluid secretions—in the saliva, for instance, or the tears, or in mucus secreted in the air tubules, or in secretions from the stomach or intestine. These seemed to be sensible places for antibodies to turn up to fight invading organisms, since bacteria and viruses often found entry into the body through moist mucous membranes. IgA was also found in mother's milk after the birth of a baby—an important point we will come back to in a moment.

Two other families of Ig antibodies might be thought of as the "little guys" and the "big guys." The "little guys" were quite small Ig protein molecules and were called immunoglobulin G (IgG). The "big guys" were larger, more complex protein molecules called immuno-

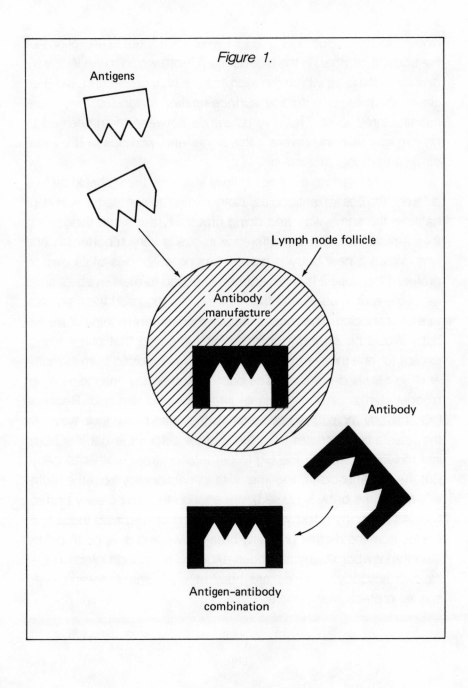

Figure 1.

Antigens

Lymph node follicle

Antibody manufacture

Antibody

Antigen–antibody combination

globulin M (IgM). Both IgG and IgM were found, not in secretions of the body, but rather, in the bloodstream. Both would make their way directly to the area where the alien invader was breaking in and then clamp themselves onto the surface-marker molecules they were manufactured to fit. The only difference between them seemed to be that IgM antibodies were a little bigger and, perhaps, a little more efficient than IgG molecules.

Immunologists are still not entirely sure why there should be two different families of antibodies, both carried to the same scene of battle in the same way and doing practically the same thing when they arrive there. But the difference in size is very important in one way. When a new baby is born, it has no antibodies of its own to protect it because it has never been exposed to alien invaders such as bacteria or viruses, and thus nothing has triggered the manufacture of antibodies. This means that for the first few months of life the baby would be an easy victim for any infection that came along, except for one thing—the Ig antibodies it has received from its mother while it is still developing. The baby's mother has antibodies in her bloodstream against all kinds of infections she has had. Because IgG antibody molecules are so small, they can make their way into the fetus's bloodstream from the mother before the baby is born. IgM molecules are just too big to get through from mother to baby. But the IgG antibodies, together with IgA antibodies from the mother's milk (if the baby is nursed), are enough to provide early protection. As the baby's first weeks and months of life pass, these antibodies from the mother gradually break down and disappear, but by then the newborn baby has been exposed to enough infection that its own antibody factories are busy at work and it doesn't need special protection any more.

Thus every normal person, from the age of a few months on, has a veritable army of his or her own Ig antibodies on hand, matched to specific alien-invader antigens or surface markers and just waiting to help fight off new infections. But where do these antibody armies come from? How does the body know exactly what shape antibody is needed in the first place? Once formed, what do antibodies actually *do* to help destroy invading organisms, other than to make them clump together and slow them down a bit? And *how* do antibodies attach themselves so perfectly to the surface of these invading foreigners? Each of these questions involves a fascinating story.

THE MYSTERIOUS
LYMPHOCYTES

The Ig antibodies do not just happen to be around in the right form
when we happen to need them. As we have seen, we have none of
our own when we are born. They appear in the bloodstream only
after an alien invader of some sort has entered the body. Then they
are literally manufactured to order with precisely the right physical
shape to clamp onto special surface markers carried by the invaders. Clearly there must be some antibody factory somewhere in the
body capable of hammering out exactly the right-shaped Ig antibodies in large quantities whenever the need arises.

In 1948 immunologists finally identified that antibody factory. Ig
antibodies, they found, were manufactured in special cells called
plasma cells scattered throughout the bone marrow and in glandlike
structures known as *lymph nodes* located all over the body. In fact,
the plasma cells themselves seemed to be formed as needed out of
other cells known as *lymphocytes*, specifically for the job of antibody-making.

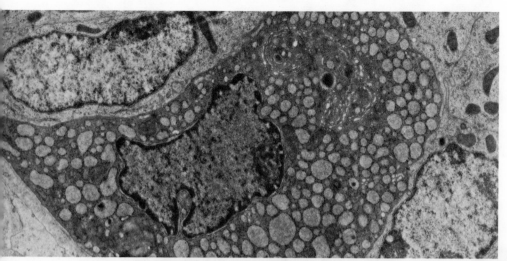

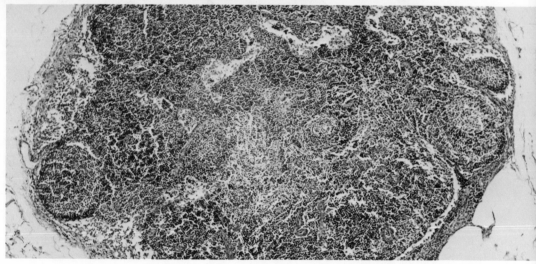

In 1948 scientists discovered that antibodies—protein molecules that destroy bacteria and viruses—are manufactured in the body in plasma cells (top picture) and lymph nodes (below).

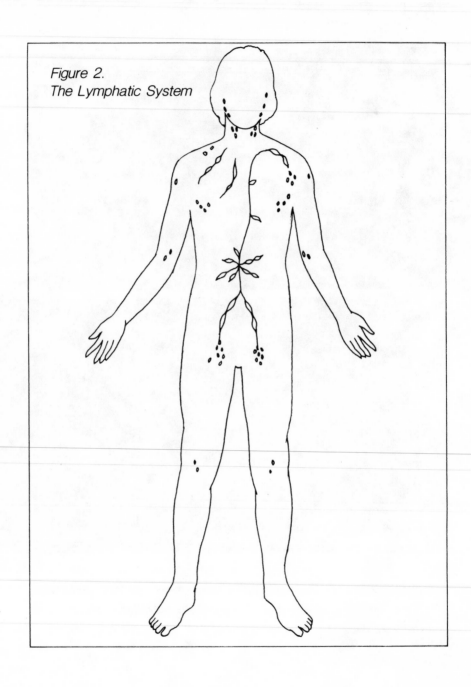

Figure 2.
The Lymphatic System

To the immunologists, this was a very important discovery. Scientists had known for years that lymphocytes existed in the body, but they really had no idea what they were there for. Lymphocytes seemed to be formed either in the bone marrow or in the lymph nodes—little glandular lumps of tissue scattered hither and yon throughout the body. Whole clusters of lymph nodes are located in the throat, for example, just beneath the tonsils, and often become swollen and tender when we develop tonsillitis or strep throat. Other clusters are found in the armpits, the groin, behind the knees, or around many of the joints. These, too, become tender and enlarged whenever an infection occurs nearby. Other lymph nodes are tucked in around the base of the lungs or the great blood vessels deep in the chest, or scattered throughout the abdomen. And the lymphocytes manufactured in these lymph nodes have long been known to find their way into the blood as another kind of white blood cell, similar to Metchnikoff's phagocytes except that lymphocytes are much smaller. Unlike the phagocytes, they seem to be made up mostly of nucleus and don't seem to devour bacteria the way phagocytes do. Ordinarily about 25 to 30 percent of the white cells in our blood are lymphocytes, but during certain kinds of viral infections, for instance, many more appear in the bloodstream.

But what did lymphocytes *do*? They didn't seem to chase and devour bacteria the way phagocytes did. In fact, they seemed to spend most of their time just drifting about in the bloodstream or traveling from one lymph node to another by way of special *lymph channels* that carry body fluids through the bays and backwaters that exist between the body's cells. It was not until the late 1940s and early 1950s that immunologist Robert A. Good and others made the startling discovery that lymphocytes were really the very foundation stones of the body's immune protective system.

SOLDIERS ON PATROL

For one thing, although lymphocytes do not seem to attack bacteria directly, they do in fact wander throughout all parts of the body constantly. Scientists have actually tagged these tiny cells with radioactive markers and then followed them in their travels. And what they do is remarkable indeed.

Carried to all parts of the body by the bloodstream, these small, pale cells wriggle and twist right through the walls of tiny blood vessels and come into contact with tissue cells in all parts of the body. They thread their way through the spaces between the cells in all of our organs, constantly meeting up with cells and body fluids everywhere, acting for all the world like soldiers on patrol in their own territory in search of enemy infiltrators. Everywhere they go they touch the special surface markers that identify every cell they contact. We can almost imagine them calling out, "Who goes there?" and then waiting for the password that indicates that the cell they have encountered is really "one of our boys," possessing the natural "self" quality that marks everything that belongs inside each individual person's own body and nobody else's. When the right password comes back—the "self" password—the lymphocyte drifts on to another cell, and then another and another, constantly challenging and testing everywhere it goes.

Presently the lymphocyte drifts into a wider fluid-filled space between the cells—the beginnings of a lymph channel. Here it is washed along into larger and larger lymph channels and finally back to a lymph node again, much the way a patrolling soldier would eventually return to headquarters to report that all was well. Then the lymphocyte goes out into the bloodstream again and travels to another part of the body to begin a similar cycle of exploration, challenging and testing and identifying the cells that it touches as "self" and therefore all right.

In each human body there are literally billions of such lymphocytes constantly infiltrating the tissues, constantly returning to the lymph nodes to "report," and repeating the cycle over and over. Unlike the red blood cells, which simply disintegrate in a few weeks, or the phagocytes, which may be killed at any moment on the field of battle, some lymphocytes seem to live a long time, perhaps for many years, patrolling the body ceaselessly, night and day.

"SELF" AND "NOT SELF"

Now suppose that a dangerous bacterial cell finds its way inside a person's body—a poison-producing streptococcus, for example, capable of causing a dangerous disease such as scarlet fever. It works its way through the soft, moist mucous membrane at the back of the throat and begins growing and multiplying, forming more and more streptococci and pouring out a toxin that damages the body's healthy tissue cells and dissolves red blood cells. Within a very short time, perhaps even within minutes, one of the body's patrolling lymphocytes comes by, makes contact with the streptococcus, challenges and tests it, and demands the password.

But this time the password comes back wrong. The surface markers carried by the streptococcus, unlike the "self" markers on the cells that belong in the body, are "not self" markers. In some mysterious way, still not really understood, the patrolling lymphocyte senses this. Somehow it "knows" that this is not "one of ours." Somehow it recognizes this cell as an enemy, a "not self" entity posing a real danger to the body, capable of killing us unless it is stopped.

(23)

However the lymphocyte may recognize this; the moment it does, its pattern of behavior changes. With remarkable rapidity it makes its way into the nearest lymph channel and hightails it for the closest home lymph node. But this lymphocyte has done more than merely recognize a "not self" enemy in the body; in some way still not clearly understood, it has also taken an accurate measurement of the invading cell's "not self" surface markers, as carefully as a dressmaker measures a woman for a dress. At the lymph node headquarters this lymphocyte is then transformed into a slightly different cell—a plasma cell—carrying the telltale measurements of the bacterial surface marker, or antigen, with it. Then, without delay, this plasma cell begins manufacturing antibody proteins to fit that specific antigen and pouring them out into the bloodstream as fast as possible.

Of course these events take time. It may be days or even longer before large numbers of formfitting antibody molecules turn up in the bloodstream or reach the site of the streptococci invasion. Meanwhile the nice phagocytes, already present in the blood and tissues, have also sensed an enemy and have gone to the attack at the infection site, trying their best to engulf the streptococci. Sometimes the phagocytes win and sometimes they themselves are killed. The poisons poured out by the streptococcal organisms may destroy hundreds of thousands or millions of white cells, so the battlefield is soon littered with dead white cells, dead bacteria, and fragments of dead body cells. But win or lose, the phagocytes may at least slow the spread of the infection until the first platoons of antibodies arrive.

To understand what happens next, we need to know something about still another weapon in the immune system armory.

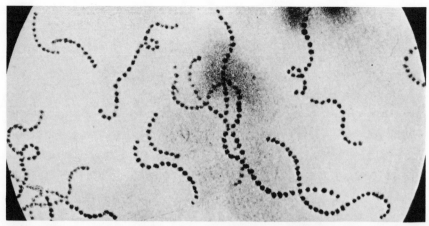

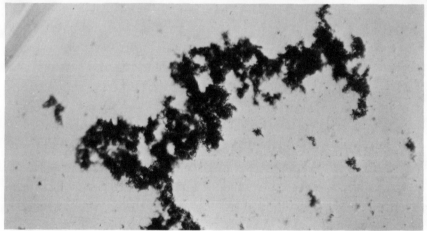

Above: a photomicrograph of streptococcus pyogenes,
*the bacteria that cause strep throat. Below: at the
site of an infection, antibodies attach themselves
to the surface marker molecules of the invading
organism, causing them to clump together.*

THE REMARKABLE ROLE
OF COMPLEMENT

When antibodies appear on the scene of infection they attach themselves to the surface markers of the invading organisms, causing them to clump together and making it easier for the phagocytes to engulf and destroy them. But the antibodies have another job to do as well. Once attached to the invader's surface they are ready to trigger one of the most remarkable chemical chain reactions to occur anywhere in the body.

Ig antibodies are really nothing more than a group of very special protein molecules. At some point in the evolution of human beings into the form they have today, another group of special protein molecules also came to be present in the bloodstream. These proteins were not antibodies; they were not formed by plasma cells, and they were not made directly in response to the presence of any foreign antigen. Rather, they were present in the bloodstream all the time, just waiting for the right sequence of events to happen.

Scientists have found that there are at least nine different forms of molecule in this particular family of proteins. These nine forms, taken together, have been given the rather odd name of *complement* because when they were first discovered it was mistakenly assumed that their job was to "complement" (that is, to help or assist) Ig antibodies in destroying invading bacteria. We now know that this was exactly backward. It is the antibodies that help or assist the nine complement molecules to fit together and transform themselves into a powerful bacteria-killer—and then point out which cell the complement should kill.

Imagine for a moment that a powerful rifle is lying on the table in nine separate pieces. Any one, two, or three of the pieces, taken alone or together, are perfectly harmless. Even all nine pieces are harmless when they are lying separate on the table. It is only when those pieces have all been assembled in the right way, in the right order, that the rifle becomes a dangerous weapon. When that has happened, the rifle is not very safe to have around—for example, it might accidentally go off or be fired in the wrong direction instead of at its chosen target.

The nine complement proteins work much like the pieces of the rifle. Once an antibody protein has clamped itself onto the surface marker on an invading cell, it provides a hooking-on place for the first of the nine different complement molecules floating around in the blood. That complement molecule provides a hooking-on place for the second complement protein, which in turn provides a place for the third to hook onto, and so forth. Only when all nine forms are hooked together in the right order does this long chain of complement molecules become armed, like an assembled rifle, capable of exploding and punching a hole in the wall of the nearest cell.

However, the complement complex doesn't care *which* cell it attacks. Any old cell will do. This would be a very dangerous situation except for one thing—the complement complex isn't strung together at all until the first molecule becomes attached to an antibody molecule clamped to the surface marker of a specific target cell. Under these circumstances, of course, with the armed complement attached to its surface, the invading enemy cell *is* the nearest cell around. The complement attached to it then becomes a cell-killer and punches a hole through the enemy cell wall, allowing fluid outside to flow in, so that the enemy cell swells up and bursts. (See Figure 3.)

This, then, is one of the major jobs that antibodies do. They assemble the ''complement rifle,'' point it at a specific target cell,

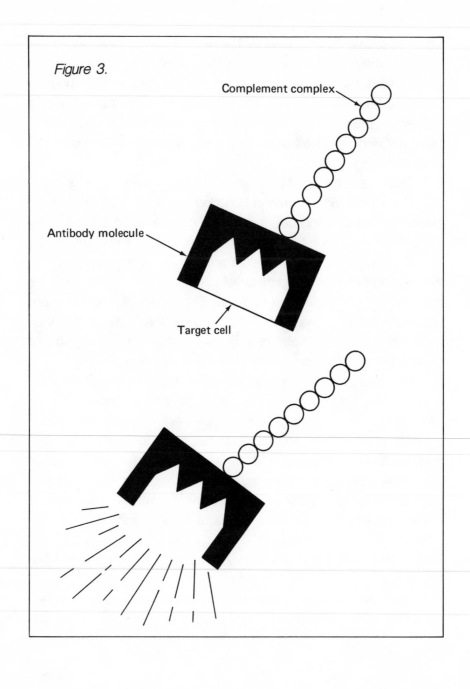

Figure 3.

Complement complex

Antibody molecule

Target cell

then pull the trigger. The invading cell is killed by the complement, while the body's own cells are protected from harm—and this peculiar battle can help put an end to infection. Faced with a swarm of specific antibody molecules working in cooperation with an efficient, deadly cell-killer like the complement, the bacteria are destroyed and the infection heals.

What is more, this part of the immune defense system provides extra protection for the future, too. Although antibodies that are not used up in conquering the infection are gradually destroyed in the body, more of the same antibodies keep being produced by the plasma cells. Therefore, some antibodies are present in the bloodstream months or even years later, ready to pounce almost instantly anytime that same alien invader should reappear. Those plasma cells also remain primed and ready to speed up antibody production whenever necessary. Thus, should an invader with those ''not self'' markers at any time in the future get back into the body again, it will be hit much faster and harder than the first time—so swiftly, in fact, that an active infection has no chance to get started at all. In some cases the only way to tell for sure that an invader has made a second attempt at infection is to discover, by lab tests, a sudden and otherwise unexplained rise in the level, or ''titer,'' of lg antibodies against that particular antigen in the bloodstream. We will come back to this point later, when we see how the process of vaccination or immunization makes it possible to build up antibody levels against certain dangerous invaders in advance, so that no active infection by those invaders ever has a chance to take place.

ENTER THE ''KILLER CELLS''

By means of the marvelous and intricate mechanism we have discussed above, the complement protein complex—triggered and aimed by antibody molecules—becomes a fiercely efficient cell-killer and thus helps the body rid itself of dangerous bacterial invasions. Everything depends on the antibodies that are formed when certain lymphocytes, warned of the presence of the invader, transform themselves into plasma cells and become veritable antibody factories. Since these lymphocytes originate, for the most part, in the bone marrow, immunologists now speak of them as *B-lymphocytes.*

But the immune system has a fascinating backup mechanism to this B-lymphocyte protective system. Certain kinds of alien invasion present such an extraordinary and real threat to our lives that the immune system has yet another form of lymphocyte to call on in these situations. These lymphocytes, which mature early in life, in the thymus gland (a lump of glandular tissue located high in the center of the chest) are known as *T-lymphocytes.* And under the right circumstances, T-lymphocytes can transform themselves into something far more grim than ordinary antibody-making plasma cells. In fact, they can change themselves into such fiercely aggressive traveling cell-destroyers that they have been nicknamed ''killer cells'' or ''killer lymphocytes.'' These potentially murderous lymphocytes are the ultimate hachet men of the immune system.

What special circumstances require the presence of these aggressive killer cells in our bodies? As it happens, certain alien invaders are very clever about the way they invade the body. Many viruses, for example, work their way inside our body's own cells and hide there. They may leave telltale ''footprints'' outside the cells in the form of foreign proteins—antigens—that indicate that they have been around, but the infectious part of the virus—its core of nucleic acid—is buried inside apparently normal cells, either forcing them to manufacture more virus particles or, in some cases, just hiding out indefinitely. Thus, in a subtle way, those normal cells have been turned into "not self" cells masquerading as "self" cells. In other cases, normal body cells may undergo certain dangerous internal changes and transform themselves into cancer cells. When this happens, whatever the cause, the usual "self" markers on those cells may alter very slightly, so that to some extent they have become "not self."

When something like this happens, the antibody-complement defense system that does such a good job of stopping a bacterial invasion may just not be up to the task that it faces. Patrolling lymphocytes may sense the presence of "not self" antigens but can't tell exactly where the danger is, because it is actually hidden inside apparently normal body cells. Antibodies may be made, but then attach to the right markers in the wrong places, so that the virus-invaded cells or the cancer-altered cells are not destroyed. In such cases the immune system takes a different course of action. Instead of stimulating B-lymphocytes to become plasma cells and make antibodies, the T-lymphocytes—apparently identical to the B-lymphocytes, yet strangely different—begin transforming themselves into killer cells, pouring out into the bloodstream and moving swiftly and directly to the invasion area. Here these killer lymphocytes recognize and surround the virus-invaded cells or the newly transformed cancer cells and launch a virulent, all-out attack. Such killer-cell attacks on altered or cancer-sick body cells have actually been photographed on movie film, and these battles actually resemble hand-to-hand combat. The killer lymphocytes start beating upon the altered cell, prodding and poking and pushing it until the altered cell's nucleus begins to change and break apart and the cell itself finally disintegrates.

In certain ways, the behavior of these killer cells, destroying cells that seem like normal body cells but really aren't, comes dangerously close to something more than just a protective system. If the killer cells were to leave some of the altered cells unharmed, the alien invader might press on and ultimately win the battle. But if the killer cells should happen to make a mistake about their targets, they might do enormous damage to perfectly normal, innocent body cells. Immunologists today believe that this actually happens sometimes and may be the underlying cause of some human diseases. But under normal circumstances these dangerous killer cells have been found to be constantly monitored or checked by other lymphocytes that have the power either to speed up their cell-killing activity, when appropriate, or slow it down, when this is indicated. Much is still to be learned about these so-called helper cells that enhance the virulence of the killer lymphocytes and the "suppressor cells" that block their activity. But the end result is a marvelously delicate balancing act, in which the killer cells are controlled like precision scalpel blades, cutting out and destroying dangerous cells while leaving truly normal cells untouched. With their activity, the immune system becomes a carefully regulated weapon to protect us from damage and preserve our lives.

4

THE IMMUNE SYSTEM AS HERO

Obviously, our bodies do not rely on a single simple immune system that always works the same way whenever the body is threatened by foreign invaders. In truth, the system is made up of several different and highly complex systems, each designed to protect the body in a different way. When an invasion takes place, all of the systems work together, but the particular part that will predominate in any given case will depend on the nature of the invader as determined by the ceaselessly wandering lymphocytes.

Each year immunologists discover more about the busy activity of this multiple protective system. Although much still remains to be learned, it is clear that the proper functioning of the immune system depends heavily on a series of fail-safe mechanisms and delicate controls that regulate all of its parts. The immune system is both very powerful and—potentially—very dangerous. As long as it works exactly as it should it is truly the hero of the body, providing us with vital life-sustaining protection against a hostile outside world. But anytime it veers off target even slightly, it can become very harmful indeed.

THE PERFECTLY
FUNCTIONING SYSTEM

What does the immune system actually accomplish for us when it is working as it should? The work it does seems more and more remarkable the more scientists learn about it.

First, as we have seen, it provides us with an aggressive first line of defense against invasions by dangerous microorganisms of all kinds. It enables us to throw off viral infections such as colds, influenza, rubeola, or mumps within a matter of a few days, usually with no serious complications or side effects. It strikes down bacterial infections caused by streptococci, pneumococci, or pertussis (whooping cough) organisms. It carries on a lifelong, running battle against the many strains of staphylococcus organisms that live on the body's surface and can cause lingering infections of the skin and underlying tissues whenever they get beneath the surface. Before we had protective vaccines, those who survived such dangerous infections as diphtheria, typhoid fever, smallpox, tetanus, or poliomyelitis did so because of the first line of defense provided by the immune system. Indeed, the immune system not only attacked the infecting organisms themselves but also provided protective antitoxins to neutralize the deadly poisons that many bacteria produced— poisons that otherwise could do terrible damage to brain or nerve cells, kidney tissue, or heart muscle.

Perhaps even more important, the immune system also provides a *second* line of defense against these major infections. Because antibodies left over after a first infection remain in the bloodstream for prolonged periods, and because plasma cells remain primed to produce more antibodies whenever necessary in the future, a person who has once recovered from a dangerous infectious disease has continuing stand-by protection against reinfection for long periods, often for life. Thus a person who has recovered from red measles (rubeola) will never have another attack because the virus that causes the disease will be stopped the moment it reappears. A person who recovers from scarlet fever will never have scarlet fever again, even though he or she may have later infections caused by other strains of streptococci. The immune system provides long-term protection against re-exposure. Add on the transfer of a mother's protective antibodies to her baby to guard it during the early months of its life, and the immune system provides protection from cradle to grave.

This protection is not confined only to protecting us against living microorganisms. We are constantly exposed to a wide variety of other foreign proteins as well, some of which are absorbed into the body. These, too, can act as foreign antigens and trigger immune reactions just as well as the protein surface markers on bacteria or viruses do. Plant pollens, animal hair or dander, protein materials from foods, bee or ant venoms, irritating chemicals such as the oils from poison ivy leaves—indeed, virtually any foreign protein material that we come in contact with—can stimulate the immune system to go into action. In many cases we aren't quite sure *why* the immune system girds up to do battle with some of these substances, since they seem to be comparatively harmless. Many of them are practically unavoidable; some are even important parts of the foods we eat. This doesn't seem to matter to the immune system. However intricate and complex its function may be, it is basically blind. It makes little distinction between a foreign protein antigen on the surface of a deadly infectious microorganism, on the one hand, and the essentially harmless antigen on the surface of a pollen grain, a molecule of wheat protein, or even a protein from cow's milk. All the immune system can do is distinguish "self" markers from "not self" markers—and any "not self" marker, however harmless it may actually be, is enough to send off the alarm. So in many cases the immune system is protecting us quite blindly whether we need to be protected or not.

VACCINATION AND IMMUNIZATION

Long before anyone even knew that there was such a thing as an immune system, physicians were putting it to work protecting people *in advance* from certain serious infections, so that they were safe from, or *immune to*, trouble when the invading organism finally did get into the body. This involves the procedure we commonly speak of as *vaccination*, or *immunization*.

In 1796 an English physician named Edward Jenner innoculated a farm boy with serum from a cowpox sore on a dairymaid's hand, and proved that thereafter the boy could not come down with the far more dangerous smallpox disease that was so widespread at the time. This was the world's first deliberate vaccination—but Jenner had no idea *why* this procedure prevented smallpox. In his day, nobody had ever heard of a virus. All Jenner knew was that people who had had the mild cowpox infection never seemed to get smallpox, even when people on all sides of them were becoming infected and dying of it.

Some ninety years later Louis Pasteur made the courageous—and very risky—decision to inoculate a boy who had been bitten by

Edward Jenner, an English physician, inoculated a farm boy with cowpox serum as a preventive measure against smallpox. This was the first deliberate vaccination, and it proved to be successful.

a rabid dog with some specially treated infectious material from some rabbits that had died from rabies. Pasteur didn't know what a virus was, either. All he had to go on was the simple observation that in many cases a person who came down with a dangerous disease, and then recovered from it, never seemed to get the disease again. Pasteur's idea was to give young Joseph Meister a "small" case of rabies in hopes that this would somehow protect him from developing a full-blown fatal case from the dog bites. Fortunately, the rabies-bitten boy lived, proving that Pasteur's inoculation technique could prevent a fatal rabies infection from occurring even after known contact with the disease had occurred.

Today, of course, we know why Pasteur's rabies vaccination worked. When an infectious organism invades a person's body, an army of antibodies is manufactured to help destroy the invader, thus allowing the body to recover. Some of that antibody army then remains in the bloodstream, ready to pounce as soon as the same invader turns up again. When a person is vaccinated against a particular disease, a small amount of harmless protein material from the infectious organism—the organism's identifying antigen—is introduced into the body. This creates a sort of mock infection that can't

Using an injection of serum on a boy who had been bitten by a rabid dog, Louis Pasteur proved that inoculation could prevent the fatal disease even after contact with the rabies virus had occurred.

actually make the person sick, but the body's immune system doesn't know that and reacts exactly as if the infection were real. Antibodies are manufactured and rush to the area of the invasion. Phagocytes arrive on the scene, ready to do battle with the invader. The lymphocyte patrols swing into action, confirming that an invasion has taken place—as far as they can tell. Presently things quiet down, after the antigen from the vaccine has been neutralized, but the immune system remains in a state of alert against that antigen. And when the real invader comes along, even years later, the immune system immediately destroys it before it can even begin to cause an infection.

The exact material contained in a vaccine will vary from disease to disease. The vaccine against rubeola, for example, is made up of real, live measles viruses that have been weakened, or attenuated, in the laboratory so that they cannot cause a full-blown case of measles. Typhoid fever vaccine contains killed typhoid fever bacilli. The surface antigen alone from the dead shells of these bacteria can cause such a powerful immune response in the body that the inoculation site often becomes sore and swollen for a day or so after the shot. Tetanus vaccine is not made from the bacteria at all, but from the extremely poisonous nerve toxin poured out by the tetanus organisms—the poison that causes the "lockjaw" symptoms of the disease. In the laboratory, this toxin is changed to a harmless form by treatment with formalin to produce a *toxoid* (a toxinlike material that lacks the toxin's poisonous qualities); vaccination with tetanus toxoid alone triggers antibodies that prevent the dangerous effects of tetanus infection. The immune response to tetanus toxoid is so vigorous that high levels of antitoxin antibodies remain in the circulation for twenty years or more.

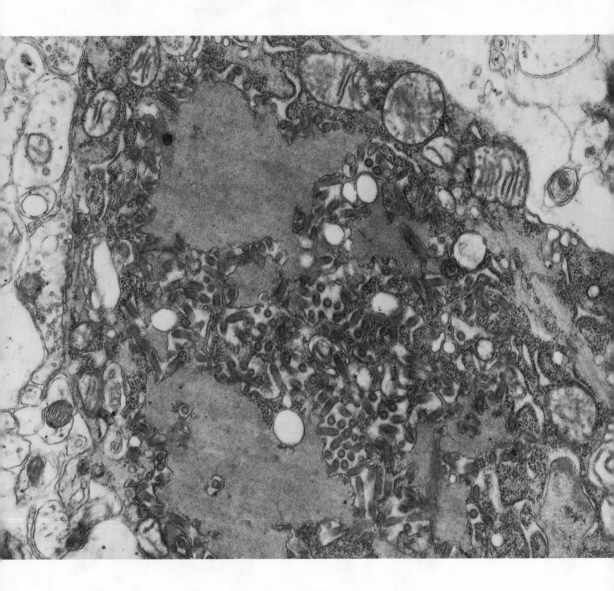

An electronmicrograph of a rabies virus

Today, in addition to those mentioned, we have highly effective vaccines to prevent diphtheria, pertussis (whooping cough), rubella (German measles), and polio, to name just a few. Travelers to foreign lands can be vaccinated against bubonic plague and cholera. One of the most recent vaccines to be developed can protect people from a dangerous viral infection of the liver known as hepatitis B.

Certainly the immune system is swift and effective in protecting the body from foreign antigens—sometimes a little too effective. It goes to work very quickly and quite blindly anytime a "not self" antigen is identified in the body. We might compare the immune system to an extremely nervous and ill-tempered farmer standing out in his field with a loaded shotgun, ready to shoot the moment he sees a suspicious-looking stranger climbing over his fence. Of course the farmer may protect his farm very effectively this way, but if he happens to be a little bit *too* nervous and ill-tempered, he may well end up shooting out some of his own windows—or even his own cow—at the same time. And strange as it may seem, this is actually very much what the immune system does, on occasion, when it overreacts to a foreign invader, or turns on the body's own normal, healthy cells—by mistake!

*Vaccinations are used
to combat a wide range of
dangerous diseases. Here
a boy is being inoculated
against smallpox.*

5

THE IMMUNE SYSTEM
AS VILLAIN

Ordinarily the immune system plays its role as protective hero quietly and efficiently, rarely calling notice to itself. Without it, our lives would be a constant and ultimately losing battle against infections of all sorts. But because of the blind, all-or-nothing way that it reacts to any evidence of invasion, there are times that it can also do harm to the body—sometimes very serious harm. There are several ways the immune system may, on occasion, take on the role of villain rather than hero. This happens by far most commonly when it works so well and reacts so vigorously to a foreign invader that the reaction itself can cause distressing symptoms. This is known as an *allergic reaction* to the invading substance.

TROUBLE WITH ALLERGIES

The immune system has no way to tell which foreign invader may be deadly dangerous to the body and which may actually be perfectly harmless. Whatever the "not self" substance may be, whether a deadly polio virus or such relatively innocent invaders as pollen grains, food proteins, or animal danders, the immune system springs into action and clears them away. What is more, after the first contact with such substances, the immune system remains alert, or sensitized, to any sign of reinvasion.

This is perfectly normal. But some people, perhaps on account of heredity, have immune systems that seem to become *abnormally* sensitive to certain of these seemingly harmless substances. In these people, when the invading substance comes along a second time, the immune system seems to react far more vigorously than normal. These people make a different class of antibodies, the IgE antibodies, in response to very small doses of offending antigens. Antibodies and lymphocytes then pour into the invasion site—and into distant tissues as well—in staggering numbers. Phagocytes come piling in, too. Fluid begins pouring out of the cells, so that localized areas of swelling occur. Worst of all, a chemical substance known as histamine, normally present inside cells all over the body, is released into the fluid spaces between the cells. Histamine causes no problem at all when it is inside the cells, where it belongs, but outside the cells it acts as a fierce chemical irritant that causes tiny blood vessels to swell, the blood pressure to fall, an outpouring of fluid into the tissues, and intense itching.

This kind of immune overreaction is rather like calling out the entire Coast Guard in order to repel one small foreign fishing boat. The end result is a so-called allergic reaction. The exact form it may take depends in part on what area is invaded by the foreign protein. When a pollen is at fault, for instance, the reaction is likely to center in the moist membranes of the eyes, nose, and upper respiratory tract. These membranes become swollen and red and begin pouring out a watery fluid. The histamine released into the tissues may cause violent sneezing and itching. This reaction is commonly called "hay fever''—probably because ragweed, which flowers during the summer haying season, is one of the most commonly offending of all pollens.

Allergic reactions to foods, insect bites, or medicines may produce a different problem—a characteristic skin reaction known as urticaria, or "hives." Large areas of the skin suddenly become red, swollen, puffy, and extremely itchy. Hives can appear while you watch them, become giant in size, and then melt into each other across the skin surface until the victim appears red and mottled all over. Then, just as suddenly and dramatically as they appear, they go away.

Another kind of allergic skin reaction, however, may take days or weeks to develop and tends to hang on much longer. This is allergic eczema. Eczema often occurs as an allergic reaction to certain food proteins, and most commonly attacks infants or children. Patches of skin behind the knees, around the mouth, in the groin, or inside the elbows, become thickened, leathery, reddened, and extremely itchy. Presently the skin breaks down and begins oozing a sticky serum that dries and crusts on the surface. Bacterial infection, introduced by uncontrollable scratching, commonly complicates the picture. Medical treatment may only partly relieve the symptoms, but fortunately, many children seem to improve spontaneously as they grow older.

Asthma is sometimes due to another kind of allergic reaction. This wheezing respiratory disorder can usually be controlled with medicines, but may recur in a chronic pattern for years in spite of treatment.

Of all the different forms of allergic reaction, however, perhaps the most frightening and dangerous is the reaction that can occur due to exposure to drugs such as penicillin, or even as a result of bee stings. In this reaction, known as anaphylactic shock, several startling things happen very suddenly and in rapid succession. The victim begins to wheeze, giant hives may appear, the eyelids grow puffy, and the membranes inside the larynx (voice box) swell up, tending to choke off the main airway. At the same time, the blood pressure suddenly drops, and the patient may faint or pass out because not enough blood is getting to the brain. This kind of shock-like reaction is extremely rare but can be very dangerous when it occurs unless it is recognized immediately and treatment is begun very quickly. Fortunately, speedy treatment with hormones such as adrenalin and cortisone, together with antihistamine drugs, can stop the reaction and reverse it almost as quickly as it comes on. Once a person has had an anaphylactic reaction, however, he or she must take great pains to avoid another contact with the offending substance. This is not too difficult with a medicine such as penicillin, but bee stings can be highly unpredictable. Today people who have had such a reaction from bee stings can be desensitized—that is, rendered less sensitive—to bee venom by means of a series of allergy shots, as protection against an unexpected violent reaction later.

In fact, desensitization can sometimes be helpful in avoiding other kinds of allergic reactions that can't be prevented any other way. The person is given by injection a series of tiny but increasingly large doses of the offending allergen (that is, the allergy-causing antigen) over a period of time. Gradually the body develops a tolerance to the substance, so that more and more is required to trigger an allergic reaction. In addition, the shots often stimulate the body to form so-called blocking antibodies, which tend to diminish the vigor of the immune reaction, like a candle snuffer over a candle flame. Desensitization works well in some cases and poorly in others; much still remains to be learned about this method of fighting allergies.

For the short term, many allergies can be prevented simply by learning from experience what substances to avoid, and then avoiding them. When symptoms do occur, they can often be relieved by the use of antihistamine drugs, which block the action of the histamine released during allergic reactions, and cortisonelike hormones, which help relieve the inflammation and itching until the reaction passes. Exactly why some people become allergic to a seemingly endless variety of substances while others have no allergies at all, nobody yet knows for sure, but heredity may play a part. The answer to this question is still just one of the mysteries that modern immunologists are trying to solve today.

HOST-VERSUS-GRAFT REACTIONS AND IMMUNOSUPPRESSION

In recent years doctors treating very sick people have run headlong into another kind of difficult problem with the immune system: It stubbornly insists upon rejecting and destroying foreign substances in the body even when the doctors, for very good reasons, don't want it to.

Since the 1940s and 1950s, there have been many attempts to prolong life by performing organ transplants—surgically removing diseased organs such as hearts or kidneys from dying patients and replacing them with healthy organs transplanted from voluntary donors or from people who have died prematurely from auto accidents or other grave injuries. Surgeons have found ways to perform such operations very successfully, and the transplanted organs function perfectly well at first. Yet most such attempts have either ended in failure altogether or have been seriously hindered because the immune system blindly and unreasoningly swings into action to reject or throw off the "not self" organ that has been transplanted.

It may be unfair to blame the immune system for doing this. After all, it is merely doing what it is supposed to do, efficiently and effectively. But organ transplants today could be saving many thousands of lives if it were not for the immune system's blind determination to "protect" us whether we want to be protected or not. To a person whose very life depends on the function of a transplanted kidney or heart, being "protected" by the immune system is small comfort.

As it is, the transplantation of virtually any organ or tissue from one person to another will be blocked by the immune system to some degree in a so-called host-versus-graft reaction or rejection reaction, unless something is done to prevent it. Such transplants, today called *allografts*, were once known as *homografts* from the Latin word *homo* meaning "same" because the grafted tissue or organ is taken from an individual of the same species. When tissue is taken from one part of a person's body and grafted onto another part of the same person—a so-called *autograft*, or "same person" graft—there is no problem with rejection because the immune system recognizes the grafted tissue as "self" and therefore "OK." Similarly, transplanting an organ from one identical twin to the other will often work well because identical twins originally developed from the same fertilized egg cell and their cells contain the same basic genetic material. In such a case the immune system of one identical twin simply identifies protein material from the other one as "self."

Fortunately, immunologists have found some clever ways to fool the immune system—or at least suppress its activity—when an allograft organ transplant is necessary. The first step is to try to find an organ donor whose cells' proteins are as similar as possible to the "self" proteins of the person to receive the transplant. If the patient doesn't happen to have an identical twin handy, sometimes a brother, a sister, the mother, or the father may have similar enough proteins that the patient's immune system will at least be confused about whether the transplanted organ is "self" or not. Immunologists now have methods for "tissue-typing" to help determine the closeness or similarity between donor and recipient proteins.

Too often, however, even the closest possible match isn't close enough, and a dangerous rejection reaction occurs after a transplant has been grafted in place. When this happens, there is only one thing to be done. The recipient's immune system must somehow be artificially suppressed or crippled—put out of commission—so that the "not self" organ can grow into place and function in peace. Powerful medicines can be given, for example, to prevent the swift growth of lymphocytes and antibody-producing plasma cells in the lymph nodes and bone marrow. At the same time, cortisonelike hormones can be given to suppress other aspects of the immune reaction. As long as these and other *immunosuppressive* treatments are continued, they will keep the transplant recipient's natural immune system inactivated and the transplanted organ can function normally. And indeed, thanks to such treatments, patients with heart or kidney transplants have survived for years. But as soon as the treatment is stopped and the immune system recovers from suppression, it usually begins once again to identify "not self" proteins and swings into action to reject the transplant. Thus, in most such patients, immunosuppressive treatment must be repeated time and again.

Unfortunately, immunosuppression itself can be very dangerous. When a person's immune system has been deliberately suppressed, it may stop rejecting a transplanted organ—but it also stops fighting off dangerous infections. These patients must depend very heavily on antibiotic treatment to control bacterial infections and must constantly be on guard against viral infections. It is because of

(50)

this terrible dilemma that only a few heart transplants are attempted today, and that development of other kinds of organ transplant procedures has been so painfully slow. Only kidney transplants are really uniformly successful. One major goal of research in immunology today is to find better and safer ways to suppress the immune system so that organ transplants can be done more often and more safely.

IMMUNITY GONE WILD:
AUTOIMMUNE DISEASES

Of all the ways the immune system can cause trouble, however, perhaps the most serious is when it starts mistaking normal "self" tissue in the body for "not self" and begins attacking normal, healthy organs and tissues as if they were some kind of enemy invader. This is essentially what happens in a number of serious disorders that doctors speak of as autoimmune, or "self-immune," diseases.

Nobody knows for sure exactly why the immune system sometimes behaves in this wrongheaded way. We do know that the immune system is both blind and terribly efficient once it has been triggered into activity. Perhaps something as yet unknown can sometimes happen to change the surface proteins on our own cells in such a way that the immune system, just doing its normal job, begins to interpret them as "not self" and blindly begins to attack them. Or perhaps, in some people, the immune system itself begins to break down in subtle ways and starts making terrible mistakes distinguishing what is "self" and what is "not self." All we really know is that when the immune system begins attacking apparently normal, healthy cells and tissues, the result can be the development of certain long-term, destructive, or disabling diseases.

(51)

The most common of these is rheumatoid arthritis, a joint disease that attacks millions of people, women far more often than men. In some people, at some point between early childhood and middle age, the immune system begins attacking tissues around the finger joints, the knees, the spine, and other joints. Huge numbers of lymphocytes appear in these joint tissues. Pain, swelling, and redness develop. Fluid fills the joint spaces, and presently a steady destruction of the joint cartilage begins. Although the disease may get better or worse from time to time, and although many medicines are helpful in relieving the symptoms, there is no known cure for rheumatoid arthritis once it has started and no way, in the long run, to prevent the crippling joint damage that slowly results in many victims.

Several other diseases are now also believed to be autoimmune. In one disabling condition known as lupus erythematosus the immune system begins damaging tissues in the skin, the blood vessels, the heart, and the kidneys. In multiple sclerosis (MS) the nerves are damaged and their function impaired, while in myasthenia gravis the muscle function is affected by an autoimmune reaction. All these diseases are still considered incurable, but vast sums of money are now being spent trying to learn more about them. Some immunologists think there may be some simple reasons for the immune system to turn against the body in certain cases, so that prevention or cure of these diseases may one day be possible. Others are not so optimistic. It may be that these diseases, when they occur, are simply the price human beings must pay for having such a complex and finicky biological system that protects them most of the time—a system that sometimes breaks down simply because it *is* so complex and finicky.

6

SOME FRONTIERS OF IMMUNOLOGY

Today immunology is one of the busiest and most exciting of all areas of medical research. The more scientists learn about the immune system, the more they realize that it is deeply involved in many everyday aspects of health and disease. It can do immeasurable good for the body, on the one hand, and serious harm on the other. Researchers today study it from both standpoints. On the one hand, they are searching for ways to enhance the immune system's natural protective function—to capitalize on the good things it can do to protect us against many dangerous and as yet uncontrolled diseases. On the other hand, they are hoping to find better ways to control the immune system in order to deal more effectively with allergies, rejection reactions, and autoimmune diseases. And in one of the most exciting and promising areas of research, immunologists today are seeking a better understanding of the connection between the immune system and the body's fight against cancer.

IMMUNOLOGY AND CANCER

Nobody knows precisely why cancer starts. Something happens in the body that causes certain cells to change into something slightly different and abnormal. Among other things, these abnormal or altered cells begin to grow and divide far more swiftly than normal. A single wildly growing cell soon becomes a cluster of sick cells, and then a lump, or tumor. Presently these abnormal cells begin to invade surrounding tissues, crowding out normal cells, and a full-blown cancer develops. At some point, cancer cells become unglued from the original tumor and travel to distant parts of the body, where they lodge and grow into new tumors. In some cases viruses are known to play a part in changing normal cells into cancer cells. In other cases pollutants in the environment, chemicals in tobacco smoke, or substances in the foods we eat may lead directly or indirectly to cancerous changes in cells.

Modern research has shown that the immune system is deeply involved fighting cancer when it first begins. It is now believed that whenever a normal cell changes into a cancer cell, the immune system somehow learns that a change has occurred and tries to do something about it. Even though the cell was originally "self" and therefore "OK," when it becomes cancerous certain subtle changes occur in its surface proteins. The immune system detects a change from "self" to "not quite self" and sets out to destroy the altered cell before it can become an actively growing cancer.

And in fact there is evidence that in most cases the immune system wins the battle. It may well be that a certain number of previously normal cells in the body are becoming cancer cells all the time, perhaps from childhood on, with the immune system searching out and destroying each one as it becomes abnormal. According to

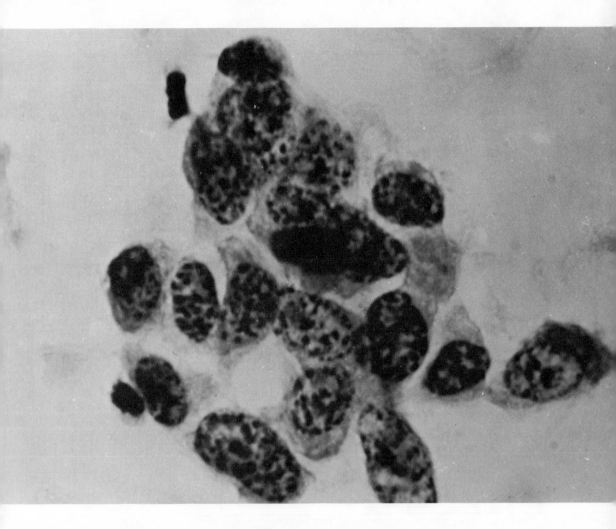

The immune system plays an important role in preventing the growth of cancer. When large numbers of normal cells turn cancerous, as these in a thyroid gland have, other means must be used to halt the spread of cancer.

this view, it is only when the immune system misses one of these dangerously altered cells that cancer has a chance to begin developing.

Even then, immunologists believe, the immune system continues the fight. It may destroy the cancerous growth at the two-cell, four-cell, or eight-cell stage of development—and it may even carry on the fight as the tumor grows larger. In some forms of cancer, killer lymphocytes are known to cluster around the cancerous growth, destroying as many of the cells as possible. In other cases, special substances produced in collaboration with the immune system seem to slow down the growth of cancer cells.

One group of such substances, discovered in 1957, are special proteins known as *interferons* because they seem to interfere in some way with the spread of viral infections or the growth of cancer cells. Several groups of interferons are now known, some of them produced by the white blood cells, some by the cells that form fibrous tissues, and some by other tissue cells. But natural interferons are made only in very tiny amounts. Experiments are now under way to see if very large doses of interferons produced in large quantities in the laboratory by means of genetic-engineering techniques (see p. 58) can be used to slow down or stop the spread of advanced cancer in humans. As we learn more about the role the immune system plays in fighting cancer, we will be able to use that knowledge to deal more effectively with this devastating group of diseases in the future.

NEW VACCINES FOR
OLD DISEASES

On another frontier of immunology, scientists are continuing the search started almost two hundred years ago by Edward Jenner to find vaccines to protect us against dangerous infections—especially some that are still very difficult to treat effectively.

Consider the problem of malaria, for example. This terrible disease of recurring chills and fever is caused by a tiny one-celled animal parasite transmitted to millions of new victims every year by the bite of infected anopheles mosquitoes. Even though malarial parasites are very definitely "not self" invaders, the immune system has never been very good at destroying these disease-causing organisms once they are entrenched in the body. For years modern medicines helped to fight malaria, but recently new drug-resistant strains of the parasite have appeared, so that more and more new malaria victims are coming down with a form of the disease that cannot readily be cured.

Faced with this situation, immunologists have been working to develop some kind of vaccine against the malaria parasite—something to stimulate the immune system in advance, so that when the parasite gains entry into the body, the immune system can do a better job of eradicating it. So far the search has been unsuccessful. It is likely that far more must be learned about how the immune system fights this parasite, and why it doesn't do a better job than it does, before this line of research can bear fruit.

The search for a vaccine against hepatitis B, a dangerous viral infection of the liver, has had a happier result. This disease, also known as serum hepatitis, is one of the most deadly of all liver infections. The virus is most commonly passed from person to person by way of contaminated hypodermic needles, drug-injecting equipment, or—in some cases—through blood transfusions. Some 1 to 2 percent of all victims die, while another 5 to 10 percent develop long-lasting or chronic liver infection after the acute illness subsides. Still others seem to get well but remain carriers of the live virus for years, capable of infecting others.

Immunologists had long been eager to develop a vaccine against this dangerous disease, especially to protect people who must have frequent blood transfusions, artificial kidney treatments, or frequent injections of medicines. But the search involved many special problems. The first task was to identify and isolate the hepatitis B virus itself. This alone took decades of work to achieve. Next, some protein marker or antigen related to the virus had to be found that could be injected as a vaccine, to stimulate the immune system into producing anti-hepatitis B antibodies. At last, just the right surface protein antigen was isolated from cultures of the virus, but in such incredibly tiny quantities and at such great expense that it wasn't practical to try to use it as a vaccine.

At this point researchers called upon a brand-new laboratory technique known as genetic engineering to find a solution to the problem. In brief, genetic engineering involves the manipulation of the genetic or hereditary material in living cells—particularly the DNA molecules that form the genes and chromosomes—in order to make those cells produce protein materials they would not normally manufacture. In the case of hepatitis B surface antigen, scientists found ways to remove DNA molecules from the interior of certain simple and harmless bacteria, break those DNA molecules apart into chunks, and then "splice" (join) segments taken from different DNA molecules that carried the "manufacturing code" for the particular hepatitis B surface protein that was needed. By using this so-called gene-splicing technique, the altered DNA could then be returned to the bacterial cells, and those cells would then begin producing the desired protein in large enough quantities to make a practical hepatitis B vaccine.

The technique worked. By "harvesting" the surface protein antigen from gene-spliced bacterial cultures, it was possible to mass-produce a vaccine that proved highly effective in preventing hepatitis B infections. The new vaccine was finally approved by the U.S. Food and Drug Administration in November 1981 and is now available for doctors to use on their patients.

There is no question that in the future immunologists will be using more and more front-line research techniques such as genetic engineering to learn more about how the immune system works, how it can be controlled, and how it can be manipulated for the achievement of better health. As just one example, a new lab technique known as *radioimmunoassay* has recently proven extremely useful for identifying and measuring the quantities of various protein substances that previously were difficult or impossible to measure at all.

The science of immunology had its faltering beginnings almost two hundred years ago, as a few medical pioneers began to realize that the human body had a built-in protective mechanism to guard it against alien invaders of many kinds. But only in the last few decades have we begun to understand how very complex the immune system really is, how beautifully it works to protect us, yet how dangerous it can be in certain circumstances. In the decades to come, further knowledge and understanding will enable us to use the immune system's natural protection more effectively—and, hopefully, to find new ways to prevent or repair the damage it can do.

GLOSSARY

Allergic reaction or *allergy*—an abnormal and often overvigorous immune reaction to an invading foreign substance or antigen.

Antibodies—special gamma globulin protein molecules manufactured to help neutralize or destroy foreign substances or antigens that have gained entry into the body.

Antigen—any foreign substance, usually containing protein, that can stimulate the production of antibodies when it gets into the body. It is sometimes called an immunogen because it *generates* an *immune* response in the body.

Antitoxin—an antibody formed to neutralize a bacterial poison, or toxin, that has entered the body.

Autoimmune diseases—diseases that arise, at least in part, when the body's immune defense system attacks normal tissue. An example is rheumatoid arthritis.

Bacteria—one-celled plantlike organisms that in some cases can cause infections.

Cancer—a type of disease in which previously normal cells unaccountably begin to grow and divide abnormally fast, forming tumors and invading and destroying surrounding normal tissue.

Cellular defense system—that part of our immune defense system made up of white blood cells—phagocytes and T-lymphocytes—that can attack and destroy invading organisms directly.

Combined immunodeficiency disease—a rare condition in which a baby is born with most or all parts of its immune defense system either completely absent or seriously impaired.

Complement molecules—special proteins in the bloodstream that work with antibodies to destroy invading foreign substances.

Gamma globulin—a family of protein molecules from which all antibodies are manufactured.

Humoral defense system—that part of the immune defense system consisting of chemical substances (antibodies) dissolved in the bloodstream and capable of neutralizing or destroying foreign invaders.

Immunity—the condition of being protected against (i.e., *immune to*) a specific infection because of stimulation of the body's immune defense system.

Immunization—the process of rendering a person immune to a disease by deliberately introducing harmless foreign substances into the body. An example is immunization of a person against poliomyelitis by administering polio vaccine containing live but weakened polio viruses.

Immunoglobulins, or *Ig's*—various forms of antibodies manufactured from gamma globulin molecules. Common forms of Ig's include IgA, IgG, IgM, and IgE.

Immunology—the scientific study of the component parts of our immune defense system and how they work.

Immunosuppressants—various drugs or chemicals that can temporarily suppress or block the activity of the immune defense system so that it cannot, for example, bring about rejection of a transplanted organ.

Interferons—special protein substances manufactured in tiny quantities by white blood cells and other tissues to interfere with the growth of invading viruses.

Lymph channels—a microscopic network of channels carrying body fluids between the cells of the body. Lymphocytes (a form of white blood cell) can move freely around the body through these channels.

Lymph nodes—small lumps of glandular tissue distributed along the lymph channels.

Lymphocytes—small free-moving cells with large nuclei that are manufactured in the bone marrow and make up one class of white blood cells. Lymphocytes play many important roles in the body's immune defense system.

Macrophages—large amoebalike white blood cells that travel through the body engulfing and destroying invading bacteria. They are one form of *phagocytes*, or "cells that eat."

Phagocytes—various forms of white blood cells capable of engulfing and digesting invading bacteria.

Plasma cells—cells in the bone marrow, derived from lymphocytes, that manufacture antibodies.

Radioimmunoassay—a complex form of laboratory test useful in identifying many different kinds of proteins in the body.

Surface-marker molecules—molecules on the surface of cells that identify, or "mark," the kind of cells they are. Traveling lymphocytes contact these surface markers to determine whether a given cell is "self" or "not self."

Vaccination—innoculation of a person with a modified virus, bacterial protein, or other substance to stimulate an immune response.

Vaccine—any serum or preparation containing an antigen that will stimulate an immune response when it enters the person's body.

Viruses—tiny microorganisms, generally much smaller than bacteria and composed of DNA or RNA within a protein envelope; these can invade body cells and cause viral infections.

ADDITIONAL READING

Asimov, Isaac. *Asimov's Guide to Science*, pp. 664–684. New York: Basic Books, 1972.

Blau, S. P., and D. Schultz. *Lupus: The Body Against Itself*. New York: Doubleday, 1977.

Glasser, Ronald J. *The Body Is the Hero*. New York: Random House, 1976.

Harris, M. C., and Norman Shure. *All About Allergy*. Englewood Cliffs, N.J.: Prentice-Hall 1969.

Nourse, Alan E. *Viruses* (A First Book). New York: Franklin Watts, 1976.

Riedman, Sarah R. *Allergies* (A First Book). New York: Franklin Watts, 1978.

Riedman, Sarah R. *Shots Without Guns: The Story of Vaccination*. Chicago: Rand McNally, 1960.

INDEX